CAMPING ADVENTURES

THIS JOURNAL BELONGS TO:

_____

IF FOUND CONTACT

HOW TO USE THIS JOURNAL

This Journal is set up to chronicle 5 different camping trips, lasting up to a week each, from start to finish.

Alternatively, you can use the daily pages for shorter trips throughout the year.

You don't have to go through the pages in order. **Feel free to jump around.**

Write, doodle, draw, color or use stickers, pictures, leaves, maps, or anything else that holds a memory to capture the moment. **Have Fun!**

WHAT IS INCLUDED?

ON THE GO

- Plan Your Camping Trip
- What Will You Take?
- What Will You Do?
- Camping Safety

CAMP ACTIVITIES

- Map Out Your Campsite
- Nature Treasure Hunt
- Camping Bingo
- Scavenger Hunt Group Selfies

DAILY ADVENTURES

- Use the Journal pages with prompts to write about your daily adventures.
- Use doodle pages for pictures, drawings, stickers and mementos.
- Use the Trip Summary pages to capture the best of your trip!

GETTING READY

I AM GOING TO

I AM GOING TO BE CAMPING FOR [ ] DAYS.

COLOR IN THE DAYS YOU'LL BE CAMPING:

MONDAY	TUESDAY	WEDNESDAY	THURSDAY	FRIDAY	SATURDAY	SUNDAY

MONDAY	TUESDAY	WEDNESDAY	THURSDAY	FRIDAY	SATURDAY	SUNDAY

WHO IS GOING WITH US:

WE WILL CAMP IN A:

what will you take?

FLASHLIGHT

MAP OF CAMPSITE

COMPASS

HIKING BOOTS AND CLOTHES

WATER

CAMERA

WHISTLE

JOURNAL

FIRST AID KIT

SLEEPING BAG

LIST OTHER ITEMS YOU WANT TO REMEMBER TO PACK:

_____   _____

_____   _____

_____   _____

THINGS TO DO

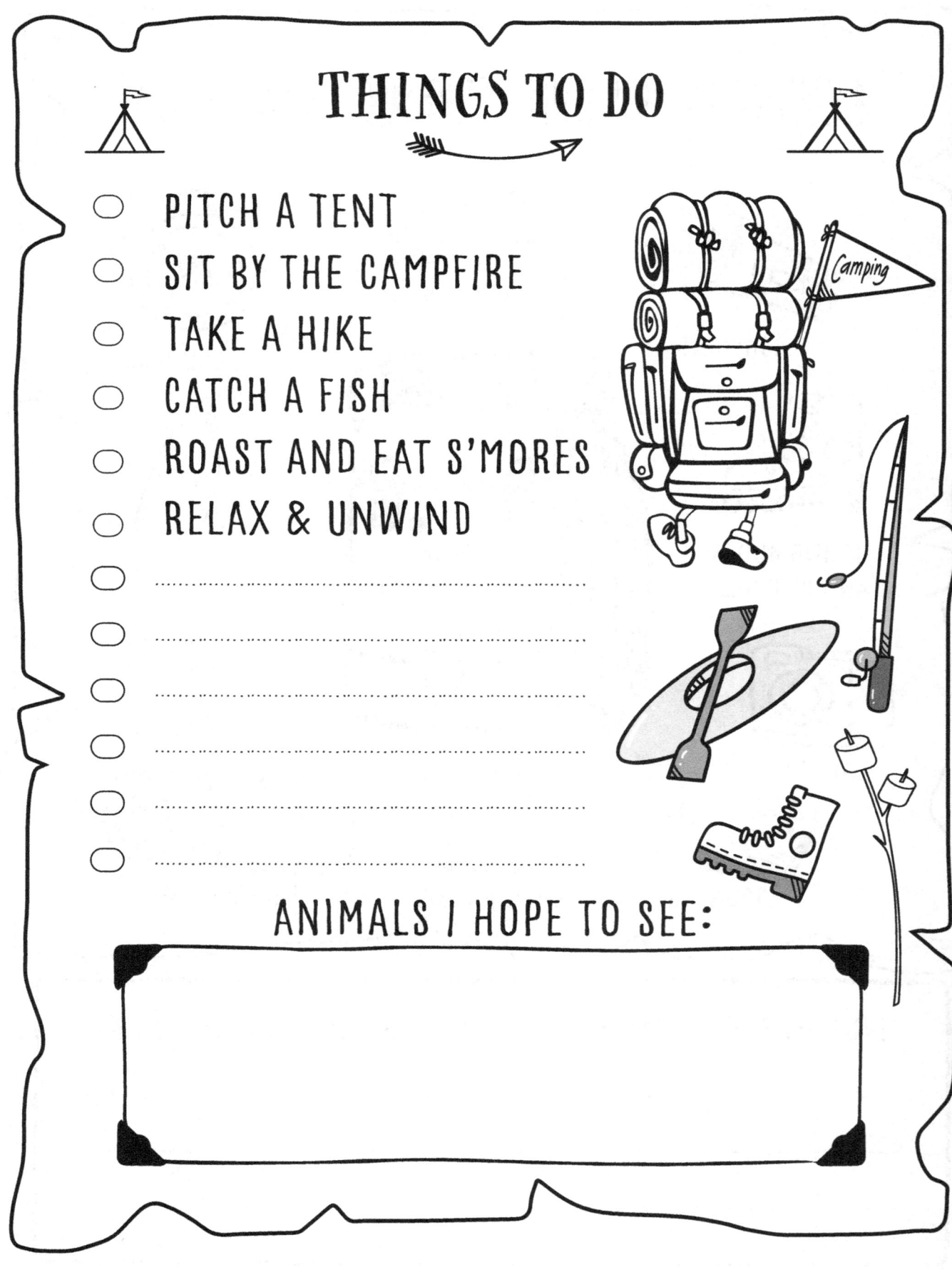

- ○ PITCH A TENT
- ○ SIT BY THE CAMPFIRE
- ○ TAKE A HIKE
- ○ CATCH A FISH
- ○ ROAST AND EAT S'MORES
- ○ RELAX & UNWIND
- ○ ....
- ○ ....
- ○ ....
- ○ ....
- ○ ....
- ○ ....

ANIMALS I HOPE TO SEE:

SAFE CAMPING RULES

→→ →→ →→

→ STAY TOGETHER ←

- STAY TOGETHER WITH YOUR GROUP.
- TELL A GROWN-UP YOUR LOCATION AT ALL TIMES.
- STAY ON THE MARKED TRAIL.
- ALWAYS WEAR YOUR WHISTLE, AND USE IT TO CALL FOR HELP IF YOU GET SEPARATED FROM YOUR GROUP.

→ STAY HEALTHY AND SAFE ←

- DON'T EAT ANY FRUITS OR PLANTS YOU FIND IN THE WILD BEFORE SHOWING IT TO A GROWN-UP.

- LEARN TO IDENTIFY COMMON POISONOUS PLANTS THAT MAY GROW IN YOUR CAMPING CLIMATE (SUCH AS POISON IVY AND POISON OAK). TAKE CARE TO AVOID THEM.

- WILD ANIMALS MAY LOOK CUTE AND CUDDLY, BUT NEVER TRY TO PET ONE.

- ASK YOUR CAMP LEADERS TO REVIEW FIRE SAFETY RULES EACH DAY. BE SURE TO PRACTICE THEM.

MY SAFE CAMPING NOTES

_____

_____

_____

_____

THINGS TO WATCH-OUT FOR IN OUR CAMPING AREA:

WATCH OUT!

Plants

Animals

Locations

Situations

camping Bingo

GET FOUR IN A ROW, UP, DOWN OR ACROSS, TO WIN

CAMPER	HOT COCOA	FLASHLIGHT	FROG
CAMP FIRE	TENT	MUSHROOMS	BINOCULAR
AXE	LIZARD	COMPASS	FISHING POLE
FISH	LOG	MARSHMALLOW FOR S'MORES	LANTERN

camping Bingo

GET FOUR IN A ROW, UP, DOWN OR ACROSS, TO WIN

PINE TREE	TREE STUMP	OWL	AXE
FLASHLIGHT	CAMP SIGN	ACORN	CAMP FIRE
BINOCULAR	HIKING BOOT	MAPLE LEAF	CANOE
COMPASS	TENT	SQUIRREL	GRILL

camping Bingo

GET FOUR IN A ROW, UP, DOWN OR ACROSS, TO WIN

CAMPER	HOT COCOA	FLASHLIGHT	FROG
CAMP FIRE	TENT	FISH	BINOCULAR
CANOE	DEER	COMPASS	FISHING POLE
MUSHROOMS	LOG	MARSHMALLOWS	LANTERN

camping Bingo

GET FOUR IN A ROW, UP, DOWN OR ACROSS, TO WIN

HIKING BOOT	TREE STUMP	FIRST AID KIT	LANTERN
FLASHLIGHT	CAMP SIGN	ACORN	CAMP FIRE
BINOCULAR	TENT	BACKPACK	AXE
COMPASS	MAP	ANIMAL TRACKS	GRILL

DRAW (OR ATTACH)
A MAP OF THE CAMPSITE.

NATURE TREASURE HUNT

CAN YOU FIND?

- [ ] 2 ROCKS
- [ ] 1 LEAF
- [ ] 2 STICKS
- [ ] 3 FLOWERS
- [ ] 1 FEATHER
- [ ] 1 BARK
- [ ] 2 PINE-CONES
- [ ] 3 BERRIES

CAN YOU SEE?

- [ ] A BIRD
- [ ] A LIZARD
- [ ] A BUTTERFLY
- [ ] A DUCK
- [ ] AN INSECT
- [ ] A FISH

LOOK FOR SOMETHING WITH THE COLOR:

- [ ] GREEN
- [ ] YELLOW
- [ ] RED

Camping Selfie
SCAVENGER HUNT

GROUP SELFIE IN FRONT OF A LARGE TREE	GROUP SELFIE HOLDING PINE CONES	SELFIE WITH TWO KINDS OF STICKS
GROUP SELFIE ROASTING MARSHMALLOWS	GROUP SELFIE SITTING AROUND CAMP FIRE	GROUP SELFIE IN FRONT OF A LAKE
GROUP SELFIE IN FRONT OF A BOULDER	SELFIE STANDING ON A TREE STUMP	GROUP SELFIE IN FRONT OF A CAMP SIGN

MY CAMPING ADVENTURES
DAILY REPORT

CAMPSITE NAME AND LOCATION:

DATE:

_____

_____

TODAY'S ACTIVITIES

_____

_____

_____

_____

WEATHER REPORT

MY RATING OF TODAY

☆ ☆ ☆ ☆ ☆

FAVORITE PART OF THE DAY

_____

_____

_____

CAMPING BUDDIES

CAMPING DOODLES

NOTES AND PICTURES

MY CAMPING ADVENTURES
DAILY REPORT

CAMPSITE NAME AND LOCATION:

_____

DATE:

_____

TODAY'S ACTIVITIES

_____
_____
_____
_____
_____

WEATHER REPORT

MY RATING OF TODAY

☆ ☆ ☆ ☆ ☆

FAVORITE PART OF THE DAY

_____
_____
_____

CAMPING BUDDIES

MY CAMPING ADVENTURES
DAILY REPORT

CAMPSITE NAME AND LOCATION:

DATE:

_____

_____

TODAY'S ACTIVITIES

_____

_____

_____

_____

WEATHER REPORT

MY RATING OF TODAY

☆ ☆ ☆ ☆ ☆

FAVORITE PART OF THE DAY

_____

_____

_____

CAMPING BUDDIES

CAMPING DOODLES

MY CAMPING ADVENTURES
TRIP SUMMARY

ONE NEW THING I LEARNED DURING THIS CAMPING TRIP:

_____

MY FAVORITE ACTIVITY WAS:

_____

BEST THING I SAW:

BEST FOOD I ATE:

SOMETHING THAT MADE ME LAUGH!

THINGS I STILL WANT TO TRY NEXT TIME:

WHAT I WANT TO REMEMBER MOST WHEN I GET BACK HOME:

CAMPING AWARDS

FIRST UP IN THE MORNING

....

LAST UP IN THE MORNING

....

MARSHMALLOW MASTER

....

BEST CAMPFIRE STORY

....

FUNNIEST MOMENT

....

MOST EMBARRASSING MOMENT

....

BEST COOK

....

_____

....

_____

....

_____

....

GETTING READY

I AM GOING TO [ ]

I AM GOING TO BE CAMPING FOR [ ] DAYS.

COLOR IN THE DAYS YOU'LL BE CAMPING:

MONDAY	TUESDAY	WEDNESDAY	THURSDAY	FRIDAY	SATURDAY	SUNDAY
MONDAY	TUESDAY	WEDNESDAY	THURSDAY	FRIDAY	SATURDAY	SUNDAY

WHO IS GOING WITH US:

WE WILL CAMP IN A:

WHAT WILL YOU TAKE?

FLASHLIGHT

MAP OF CAMPSITE

COMPASS

HIKING BOOTS AND CLOTHES

H2O

WATER

CAMERA

WHISTLE

JOURNAL

FIRST AID KIT

SLEEPING BAG

LIST OTHER ITEMS YOU WANT TO REMEMBER TO PACK:

_____   _____

_____   _____

_____

THINGS TO DO

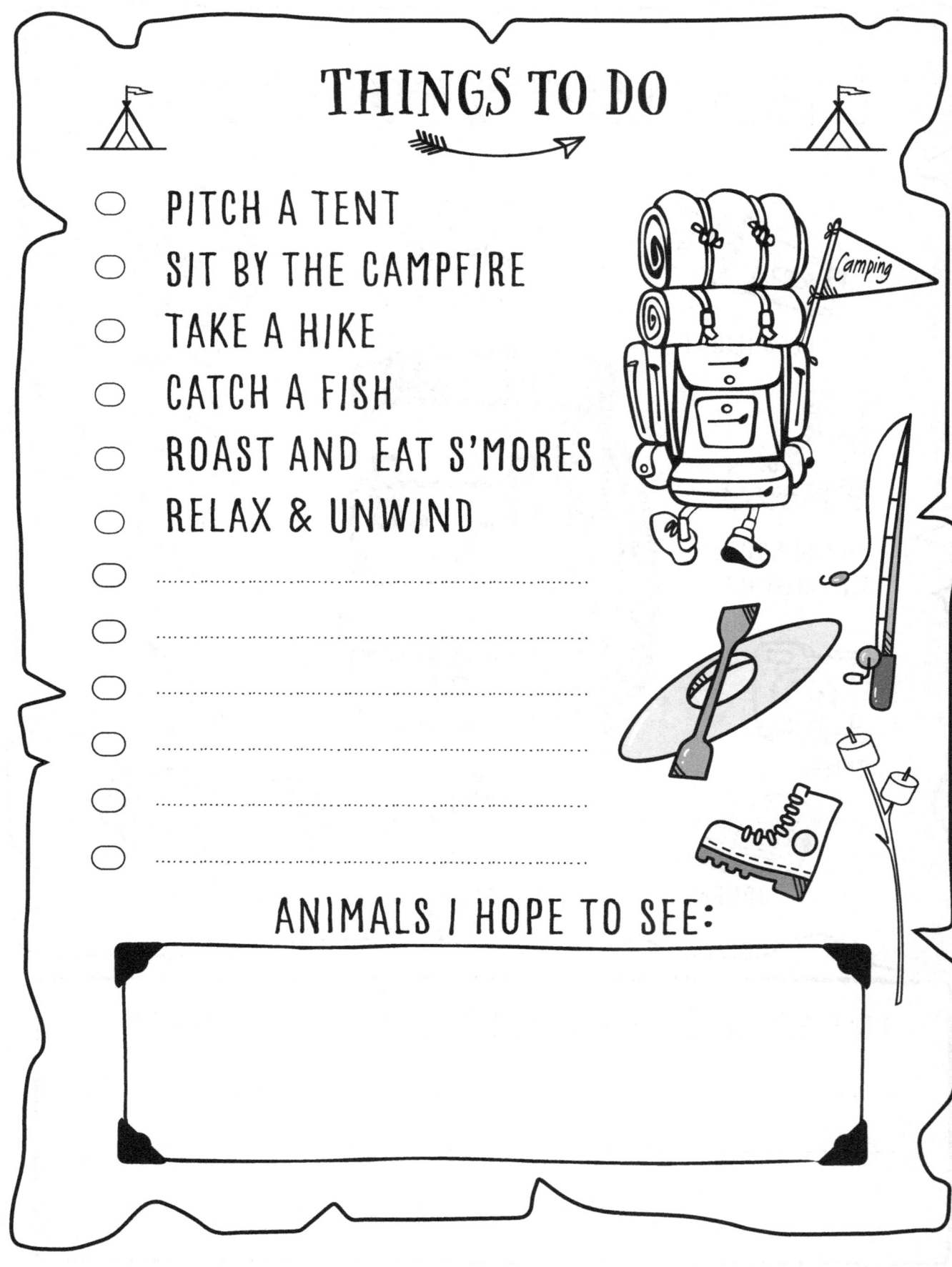

- ○ PITCH A TENT
- ○ SIT BY THE CAMPFIRE
- ○ TAKE A HIKE
- ○ CATCH A FISH
- ○ ROAST AND EAT S'MORES
- ○ RELAX & UNWIND
- ○ ....
- ○ ....
- ○ ....
- ○ ....
- ○ ....
- ○ ....

ANIMALS I HOPE TO SEE:

SAFE CAMPING RULES

STAY TOGETHER

- STAY TOGETHER WITH YOUR GROUP.
- TELL A GROWN-UP YOUR LOCATION AT ALL TIMES.
- STAY ON THE MARKED TRAIL.
- ALWAYS WEAR YOUR WHISTLE, AND USE IT TO CALL FOR HELP IF YOU GET SEPARATED FROM YOUR GROUP.

STAY HEALTHY AND SAFE

- DON'T EAT ANY FRUITS OR PLANTS YOU FIND IN THE WILD BEFORE SHOWING IT TO A GROWN-UP.
- LEARN TO IDENTIFY COMMON POISONOUS PLANTS THAT MAY GROW IN YOUR CAMPING CLIMATE (SUCH AS POISON IVY AND POISON OAK). TAKE CARE TO AVOID THEM.
- WILD ANIMALS MAY LOOK CUTE AND CUDDLY, BUT NEVER TRY TO PET ONE.
- ASK YOUR CAMP LEADERS TO REVIEW FIRE SAFETY RULES EACH DAY. BE SURE TO PRACTICE THEM.

MY SAFE CAMPING NOTES

_____

_____

_____

_____

THINGS TO WATCH-OUT FOR IN OUR CAMPING AREA:

WATCH OUT!

Plants	Animals

Locations	Situations

camping Bingo

GET FOUR IN A ROW, UP, DOWN OR ACROSS, TO WIN

CAMPER	HOT COCOA	FLASHLIGHT	FROG
CAMP FIRE	TENT	MUSHROOMS	BINOCULAR
AXE	LIZARD	COMPASS	FISHING POLE
FISH	LOG	MARSHMALLOW FOR S'MORES	LANTERN

camping bingo

GET FOUR IN A ROW, UP, DOWN OR ACROSS, TO WIN

PINE TREE	TREE STUMP	OWL	AXE
FLASHLIGHT	CAMP SIGN	ACORN	CAMP FIRE
BINOCULAR	HIKING BOOT	MAPLE LEAF	CANOE
COMPASS	TENT	SQUIRREL	GRILL

camping Bingo

GET FOUR IN A ROW, UP, DOWN OR ACROSS, TO WIN

CAMPER	HOT COCOA	FLASHLIGHT	FROG
CAMP FIRE	TENT	FISH	BINOCULAR
CANOE	DEER	COMPASS	FISHING POLE
MUSHROOMS	LOG	MARSHMALLOWS	LANTERN

camping Bingo

GET FOUR IN A ROW, UP, DOWN OR ACROSS, TO WIN

HIKING BOOT	TREE STUMP	FIRST AID KIT	LANTERN
FLASHLIGHT	CAMP SIGN	ACORN	CAMP FIRE
BINOCULAR	TENT	BACKPACK	AXE
COMPASS	MAP	ANIMAL TRACKS	GRILL

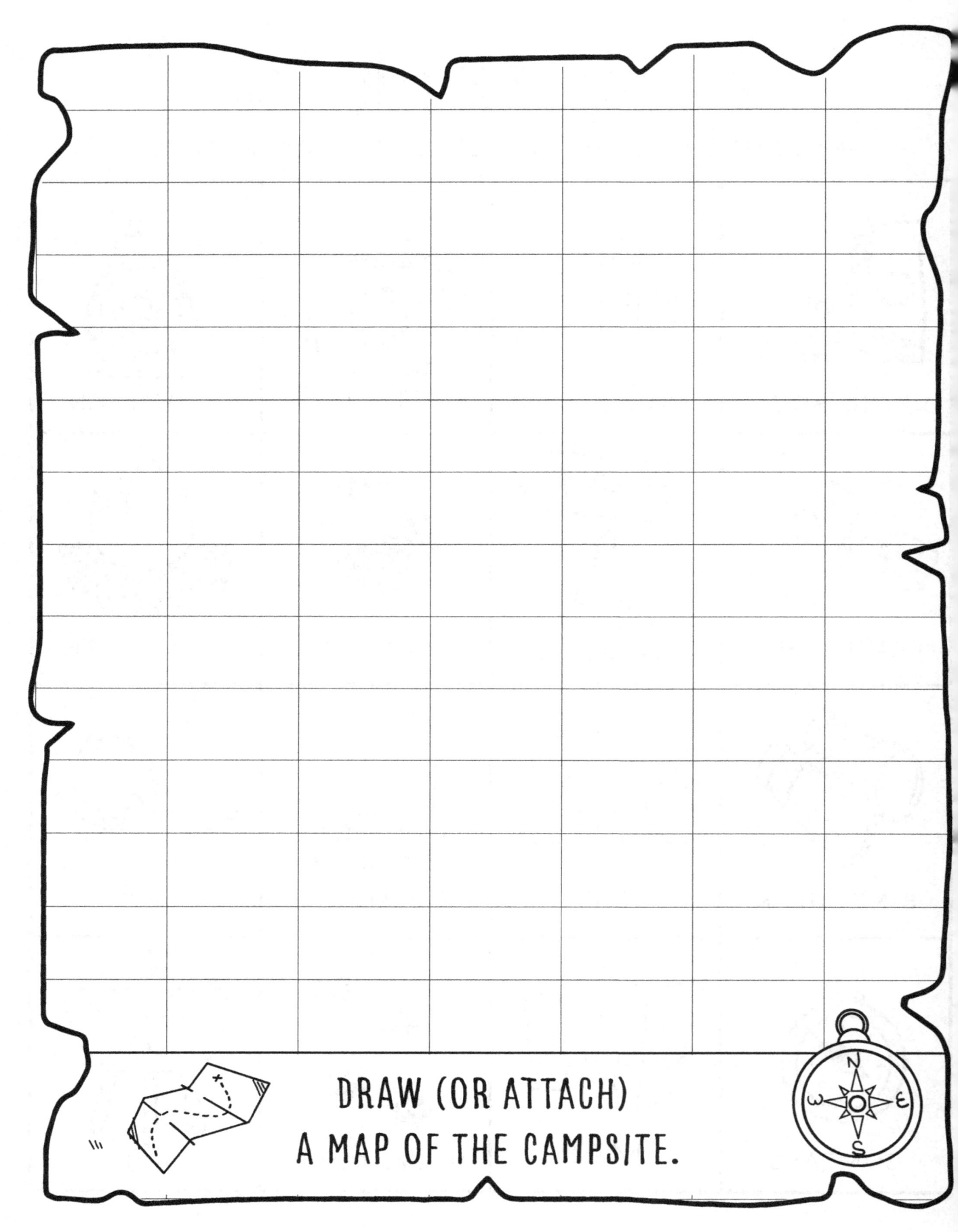

DRAW (OR ATTACH)
A MAP OF THE CAMPSITE.

NATURE TREASURE HUNT

CAN YOU FIND?

- [ ] 2 ROCKS
- [ ] 1 LEAF
- [ ] 2 STICKS
- [ ] 3 FLOWERS
- [ ] 1 FEATHER
- [ ] 1 BARK
- [ ] 2 PINE-CONES
- [ ] 3 BERRIES

CAN YOU SEE?

- [ ] A BIRD
- [ ] A LIZARD
- [ ] A BUTTERFLY
- [ ] A DUCK
- [ ] AN INSECT
- [ ] A FISH

LOOK FOR SOMETHING WITH THE COLOR:

- [ ] GREEN
- [ ] YELLOW
- [ ] RED

Camping  Selfie
SCAVENGER HUNT

GROUP SELFIE IN FRONT OF A LARGE TREE	GROUP SELFIE HOLDING PINE CONES	SELFIE WITH TWO KINDS OF STICKS
GROUP SELFIE ROASTING MARSHMALLOWS	GROUP SELFIE SITTING AROUND CAMP FIRE	GROUP SELFIE IN FRONT OF A LAKE
GROUP SELFIE IN FRONT OF A BOULDER	SELFIE STANDING ON A TREE STUMP	GROUP SELFIE IN FRONT OF A CAMP SIGN

MY CAMPING ADVENTURES
DAILY REPORT

CAMPSITE NAME AND LOCATION:

_____

DATE:

_____

TODAY'S ACTIVITIES

_____

_____

_____

_____

WEATHER REPORT

MY RATING OF TODAY

☆ ☆ ☆ ☆ ☆

FAVORITE PART OF THE DAY

_____

_____

_____

CAMPING BUDDIES

CAMPING DOODLES

NOTES AND PICTURES

MY CAMPING ADVENTURES
DAILY REPORT

CAMPSITE NAME AND LOCATION:

DATE:

_____ _____

TODAY'S ACTIVITIES

_____

_____

_____

_____

WEATHER REPORT

MY RATING OF TODAY

☆ ☆ ☆ ☆ ☆

FAVORITE PART OF THE DAY

_____

_____

_____

CAMPING BUDDIES

MY CAMPING ADVENTURES
DAILY REPORT

CAMPSITE NAME AND LOCATION:

_____

DATE:

_____

TODAY'S ACTIVITIES

_____

_____

_____

_____

WEATHER REPORT

MY RATING OF TODAY

☆ ☆ ☆ ☆ ☆

FAVORITE PART OF THE DAY

_____

_____

_____

CAMPING BUDDIES

CAMPING DOODLES

MY CAMPING ADVENTURES
TRIP SUMMARY

ONE NEW THING I LEARNED DURING THIS CAMPING TRIP:

MY FAVORITE ACTIVITY WAS:

BEST THING I SAW:

BEST FOOD I ATE:

SOMETHING THAT MADE ME LAUGH!

THINGS I STILL WANT TO TRY NEXT TIME:

WHAT I WANT TO REMEMBER MOST WHEN I GET BACK HOME:

CAMPING AWARDS

FIRST UP IN THE MORNING	**LAST UP IN THE MORNING**
....	....
MARSHMALLOW MASTER	**BEST CAMPFIRE STORY**
....	....
FUNNIEST MOMENT	**MOST EMBARRASSING MOMENT**
....	....
BEST COOK	_____
....	....
_____	_____
....	....

GETTING READY

I AM GOING TO [   ]

I AM GOING TO BE CAMPING FOR [   ] DAYS.

COLOR IN THE DAYS YOU'LL BE CAMPING:

MONDAY	TUESDAY	WEDNESDAY	THURSDAY	FRIDAY	SATURDAY	SUNDAY
MONDAY	TUESDAY	WEDNESDAY	THURSDAY	FRIDAY	SATURDAY	SUNDAY

WHO IS GOING WITH US:

WE WILL CAMP IN A:

What Will You Take?

FLASHLIGHT

MAP OF CAMPSITE

COMPASS

HIKING BOOTS
AND CLOTHES

WATER

CAMERA

WHISTLE

JOURNAL

FIRST AID KIT

SLEEPING BAG

LIST OTHER ITEMS YOU WANT TO REMEMBER TO PACK:

_____   _____

_____   _____

_____   _____

THINGS TO DO

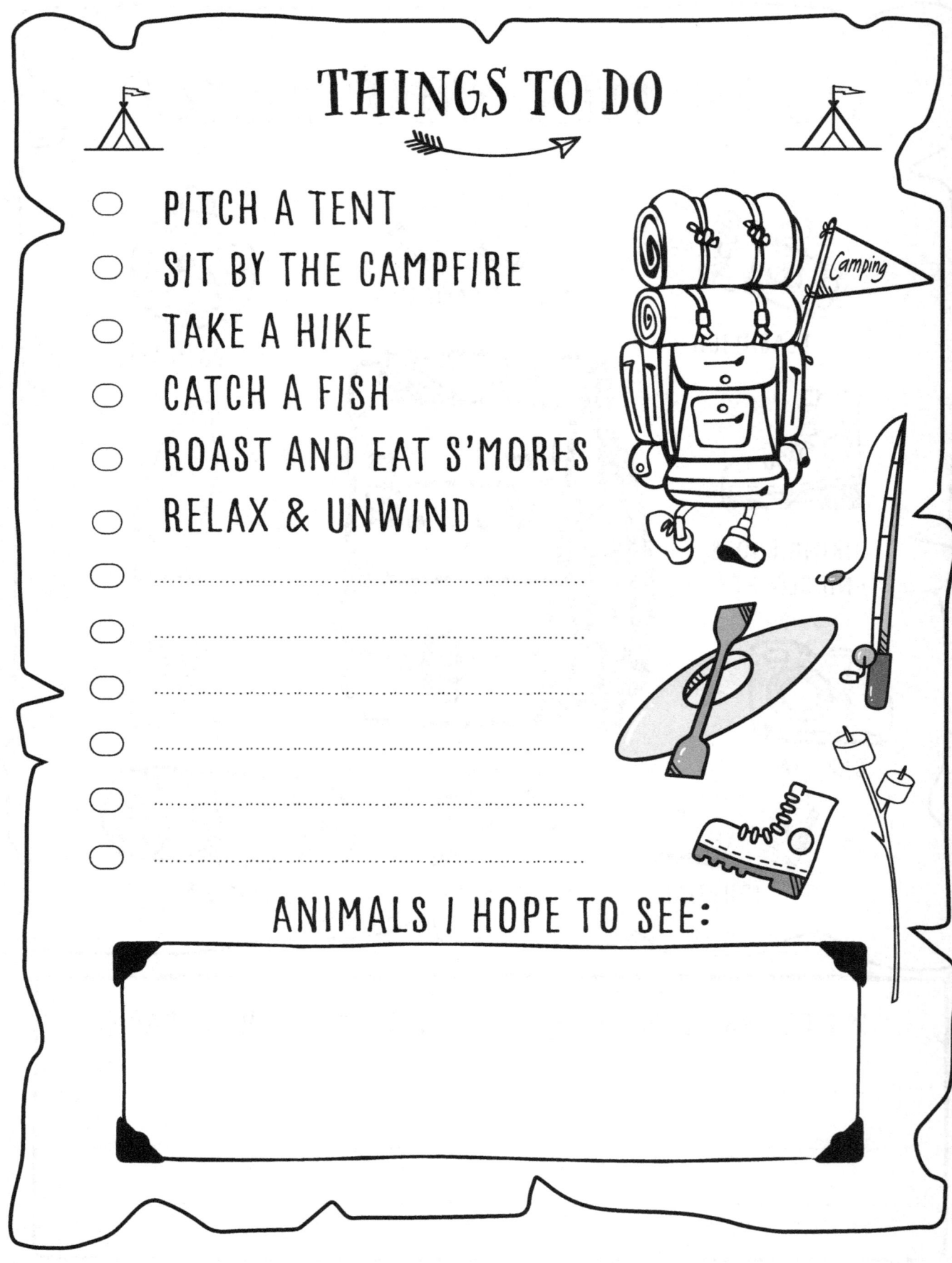

- ○ PITCH A TENT
- ○ SIT BY THE CAMPFIRE
- ○ TAKE A HIKE
- ○ CATCH A FISH
- ○ ROAST AND EAT S'MORES
- ○ RELAX & UNWIND
- ○ ....
- ○ ....
- ○ ....
- ○ ....
- ○ ....
- ○ ....

ANIMALS I HOPE TO SEE:

safe camping Rules

→ STAY TOGETHER ←

- STAY TOGETHER WITH YOUR GROUP.
- TELL A GROWN-UP YOUR LOCATION AT ALL TIMES.
- STAY ON THE MARKED TRAIL.
- ALWAYS WEAR YOUR WHISTLE, AND USE IT TO CALL FOR HELP IF YOU GET SEPARATED FROM YOUR GROUP.

→ STAY HEALTHY AND SAFE ←

- DON'T EAT ANY FRUITS OR PLANTS YOU FIND IN THE WILD BEFORE SHOWING IT TO A GROWN-UP.

- LEARN TO IDENTIFY COMMON POISONOUS PLANTS THAT MAY GROW IN YOUR CAMPING CLIMATE (SUCH AS POISON IVY AND POISON OAK). TAKE CARE TO AVOID THEM.

- WILD ANIMALS MAY LOOK CUTE AND CUDDLY, BUT NEVER TRY TO PET ONE.

- ASK YOUR CAMP LEADERS TO REVIEW FIRE SAFETY RULES EACH DAY. BE SURE TO PRACTICE THEM.

FOREST
CABIN
LAKE

MY SAFE CAMPING NOTES

_____

_____

_____

_____

THINGS TO WATCH-OUT FOR IN OUR CAMPING AREA:

WATCH OUT!

Plants	Animals

Locations	Situations

camping bingo

GET FOUR IN A ROW, UP, DOWN OR ACROSS, TO WIN

CAMPER	HOT COCOA	FLASHLIGHT	FROG
CAMP FIRE	TENT	MUSHROOMS	BINOCULAR
AXE	LIZARD	COMPASS	FISHING POLE
FISH	LOG	MARSHMALLOW FOR S'MORES	LANTERN

camping bingo

GET FOUR IN A ROW, UP, DOWN OR ACROSS, TO WIN

PINE TREE	TREE STUMP	OWL	AXE
FLASHLIGHT	CAMP SIGN	ACORN	CAMP FIRE
BINOCULAR	HIKING BOOT	MAPLE LEAF	CANOE
COMPASS	TENT	SQUIRREL	GRILL

camping bingo

GET FOUR IN A ROW, UP, DOWN OR ACROSS, TO WIN

CAMPER	HOT COCOA	FLASHLIGHT	FROG
CAMP FIRE	TENT	FISH	BINOCULAR
CANOE	DEER	COMPASS	FISHING POLE
MUSHROOMS	LOG	MARSHMALLOWS	LANTERN

camping bingo

GET FOUR IN A ROW, UP, DOWN OR ACROSS, TO WIN

HIKING BOOT	TREE STUMP	FIRST AID KIT	LANTERN
FLASHLIGHT	CAMP SIGN	ACORN	CAMP FIRE
BINOCULAR	TENT	BACKPACK	AXE
COMPASS	MAP	ANIMAL TRACKS	GRILL

DRAW (OR ATTACH)
A MAP OF THE CAMPSITE.

NATURE TREASURE HUNT

CAN YOU FIND?

- ☐ 2 ROCKS
- ☐ 1 LEAF
- ☐ 2 STICKS
- ☐ 3 FLOWERS
- ☐ 1 FEATHER
- ☐ 1 BARK
- ☐ 2 PINE-CONES
- ☐ 3 BERRIES

CAN YOU SEE?

- ☐ A BIRD
- ☐ A LIZARD
- ☐ A BUTTERFLY
- ☐ A DUCK
- ☐ AN INSECT
- ☐ A FISH

LOOK FOR SOMETHING WITH THE COLOR:

- ☐ GREEN
- ☐ YELLOW
- ☐ RED

Camping Selfie

SCAVENGER HUNT

GROUP SELFIE IN FRONT OF A LARGE TREE

GROUP SELFIE HOLDING PINE CONES

SELFIE WITH TWO KINDS OF STICKS

GROUP SELFIE ROASTING MARSHMALLOWS

GROUP SELFIE SITTING AROUND CAMP FIRE

GROUP SELFIE IN FRONT OF A LAKE

GROUP SELFIE IN FRONT OF A BOULDER

SELFIE STANDING ON A TREE STUMP

GROUP SELFIE IN FRONT OF A CAMP SIGN

MY CAMPING ADVENTURES
DAILY REPORT

CAMPSITE NAME AND LOCATION:

DATE:

_____

_____

TODAY'S ACTIVITIES

_____

_____

_____

WEATHER REPORT

MY RATING OF TODAY

☆ ☆ ☆ ☆ ☆

FAVORITE PART OF THE DAY

_____

_____

_____

CAMPING BUDDIES

CAMPING DOODLES

NOTES AND PICTURES

MY CAMPING ADVENTURES
DAILY REPORT

CAMPSITE NAME AND LOCATION:

DATE:

_____ _____

TODAY'S ACTIVITIES

_____

_____

_____

_____

WEATHER REPORT

MY RATING OF TODAY

FAVORITE PART OF THE DAY

_____

_____

_____

CAMPING BUDDIES

MY CAMPING ADVENTURES
DAILY REPORT

CAMPSITE NAME AND LOCATION:

_____

DATE:

_____

TODAY'S ACTIVITIES

_____

_____

_____

_____

WEATHER REPORT

MY RATING OF TODAY

☆ ☆ ☆ ☆ ☆

FAVORITE PART OF THE DAY

_____

_____

_____

CAMPING BUDDIES

CAMPING DOODLES

MY CAMPING ADVENTURES
TRIP SUMMARY

ONE NEW THING I LEARNED DURING THIS CAMPING TRIP:

_____

MY FAVORITE ACTIVITY WAS:

_____

BEST THING I SAW:

BEST FOOD I ATE:

SOMETHING THAT MADE ME LAUGH!

THINGS I STILL WANT TO TRY NEXT TIME:

WHAT I WANT TO REMEMBER MOST WHEN I GET BACK HOME:

Camping Awards

FIRST UP IN THE MORNING

....

LAST UP IN THE MORNING

....

MARSHMALLOW MASTER

....

BEST CAMPFIRE STORY

....

FUNNIEST MOMENT

....

MOST EMBARRASSING MOMENT

....

BEST COOK

....

_____

....

_____

....

_____

....

GETTING READY

I AM GOING TO [_____]

I AM GOING TO BE CAMPING FOR [____] DAYS.

COLOR IN THE DAYS YOU'LL BE CAMPING:

MONDAY	TUESDAY	WEDNESDAY	THURSDAY	FRIDAY	SATURDAY	SUNDAY

MONDAY	TUESDAY	WEDNESDAY	THURSDAY	FRIDAY	SATURDAY	SUNDAY

WHO IS GOING WITH US:

WE WILL CAMP IN A:

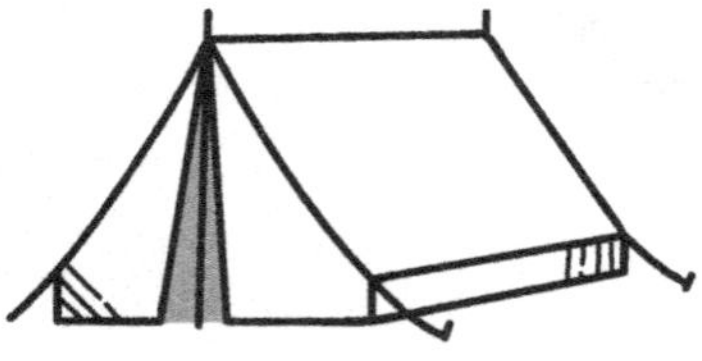

what will you take?

FLASHLIGHT

MAP OF CAMPSITE

COMPASS

HIKING BOOTS
AND CLOTHES

WATER

CAMERA

WHISTLE

JOURNAL

FIRST AID KIT

SLEEPING BAG

LIST OTHER ITEMS YOU WANT TO REMEMBER TO PACK:

_____   _____

_____   _____

_____   _____

THINGS TO DO

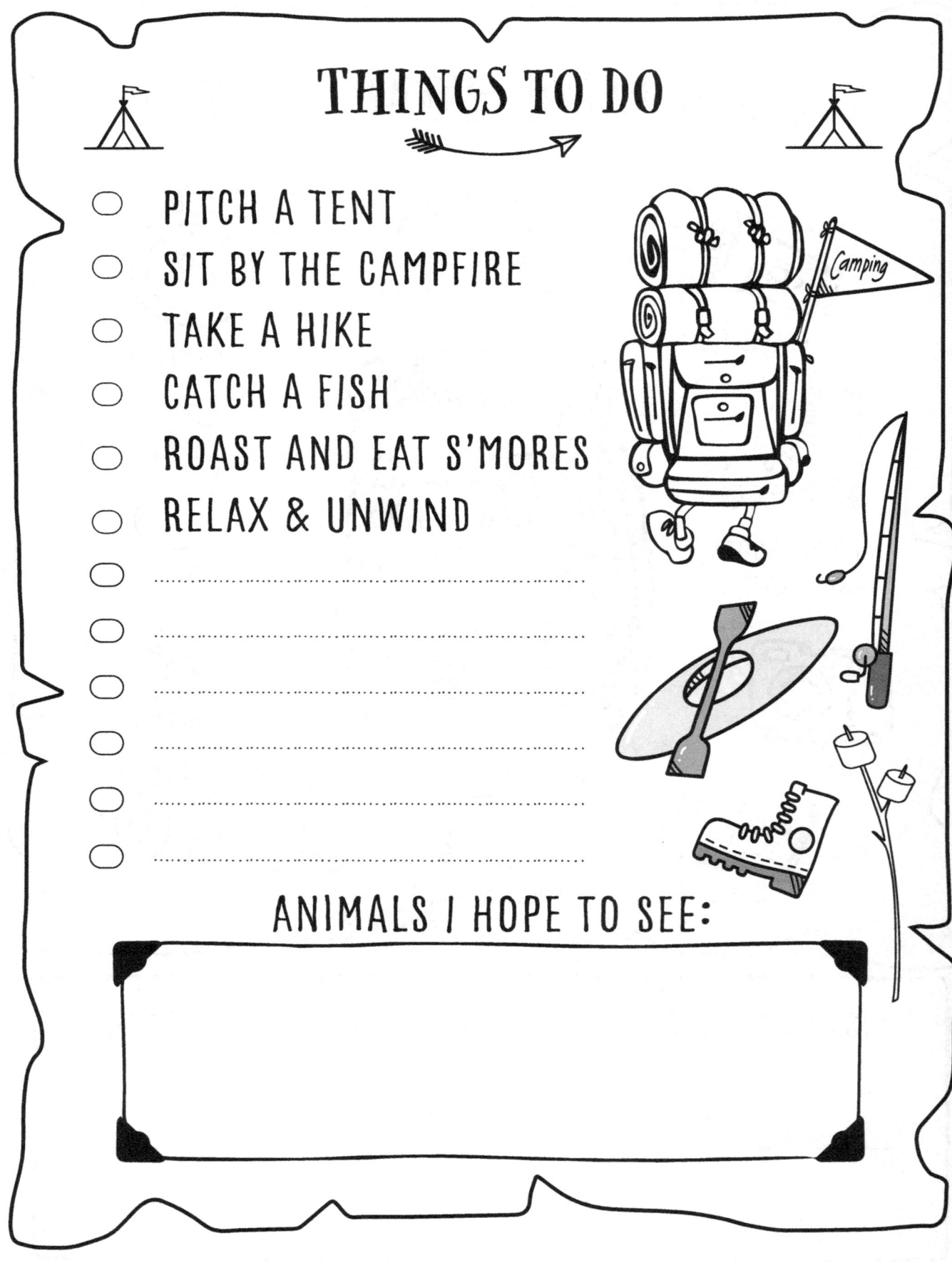

- ○ PITCH A TENT
- ○ SIT BY THE CAMPFIRE
- ○ TAKE A HIKE
- ○ CATCH A FISH
- ○ ROAST AND EAT S'MORES
- ○ RELAX & UNWIND
- ○ ....
- ○ ....
- ○ ....
- ○ ....
- ○ ....
- ○ ....

ANIMALS I HOPE TO SEE:

Safe Camping Rules

→ STAY TOGETHER ←

- STAY TOGETHER WITH YOUR GROUP.
- TELL A GROWN-UP YOUR LOCATION AT ALL TIMES.
- STAY ON THE MARKED TRAIL.
- ALWAYS WEAR YOUR WHISTLE, AND USE IT TO CALL FOR HELP IF YOU GET SEPARATED FROM YOUR GROUP.

FOREST
CABIN
LAKE

→ STAY HEALTHY AND SAFE ←

- DON'T EAT ANY FRUITS OR PLANTS YOU FIND IN THE WILD BEFORE SHOWING IT TO A GROWN-UP.
- LEARN TO IDENTIFY COMMON POISONOUS PLANTS THAT MAY GROW IN YOUR CAMPING CLIMATE (SUCH AS POISON IVY AND POISON OAK). TAKE CARE TO AVOID THEM.
- WILD ANIMALS MAY LOOK CUTE AND CUDDLY, BUT NEVER TRY TO PET ONE.
- ASK YOUR CAMP LEADERS TO REVIEW FIRE SAFETY RULES EACH DAY. BE SURE TO PRACTICE THEM.

MY SAFE CAMPING NOTES

_____

_____

_____

_____

THINGS TO WATCH-OUT FOR
IN OUR CAMPING AREA:

WATCH OUT!

Plants	Animals

Locations	Situations

camping bingo

GET FOUR IN A ROW, UP, DOWN OR ACROSS, TO WIN

CAMPER	HOT COCOA	FLASHLIGHT	FROG
CAMP FIRE	TENT	MUSHROOMS	BINOCULAR
AXE	LIZARD	COMPASS	FISHING POLE
FISH	LOG	MARSHMALLOW FOR S'MORES	LANTERN

camping bingo

GET FOUR IN A ROW, UP, DOWN OR ACROSS, TO WIN

PINE TREE	TREE STUMP	OWL	AXE
FLASHLIGHT	CAMP SIGN	ACORN	CAMP FIRE
BINOCULAR	HIKING BOOT	MAPLE LEAF	CANOE
COMPASS	TENT	SQUIRREL	GRILL

camping bingo

GET FOUR IN A ROW, UP, DOWN OR ACROSS, TO WIN

CAMPER	HOT COCOA	FLASHLIGHT	FROG
CAMP FIRE	TENT	FISH	BINOCULAR
CANOE	DEER	COMPASS	FISHING POLE
MUSHROOMS	LOG	MARSHMALLOWS	LANTERN

camping Bingo

GET FOUR IN A ROW, UP, DOWN OR ACROSS, TO WIN

HIKING BOOT	TREE STUMP	FIRST AID KIT	LANTERN
FLASHLIGHT	CAMP SIGN	ACORN	CAMP FIRE
BINOCULAR	TENT	BACKPACK	AXE
COMPASS	MAP	ANIMAL TRACKS	GRILL

DRAW (OR ATTACH)
A MAP OF THE CAMPSITE.

NATURE TREASURE HUNT

CAN YOU FIND?

- [ ] 2 ROCKS
- [ ] 1 LEAF
- [ ] 2 STICKS
- [ ] 3 FLOWERS
- [ ] 1 FEATHER
- [ ] 1 BARK
- [ ] 2 PINE-CONES
- [ ] 3 BERRIES

CAN YOU SEE?

- [ ] A BIRD
- [ ] A LIZARD
- [ ] A BUTTERFLY
- [ ] A DUCK
- [ ] AN INSECT
- [ ] A FISH

LOOK FOR SOMETHING WITH THE COLOR:

- [ ] GREEN
- [ ] YELLOW
- [ ] RED

Camping selfie
SCAVENGER HUNT

GROUP SELFIE IN FRONT OF A LARGE TREE	GROUP SELFIE HOLDING PINE CONES	SELFIE WITH TWO KINDS OF STICKS
GROUP SELFIE ROASTING MARSHMALLOWS	GROUP SELFIE SITTING AROUND CAMP FIRE	GROUP SELFIE IN FRONT OF A LAKE
GROUP SELFIE IN FRONT OF A BOULDER	SELFIE STANDING ON A TREE STUMP	GROUP SELFIE IN FRONT OF A CAMP SIGN

MY CAMPING ADVENTURES
DAILY REPORT

CAMPSITE NAME AND LOCATION:

DATE:

_____

_____

TODAY'S ACTIVITIES

_____

_____

_____

_____

WEATHER REPORT

MY RATING OF TODAY

FAVORITE PART OF THE DAY

_____

_____

_____

CAMPING BUDDIES

CAMPING DOODLES

NOTES AND PICTURES

MY CAMPING ADVENTURES
DAILY REPORT

CAMPSITE NAME AND LOCATION:

DATE:

_____

_____

TODAY'S ACTIVITIES

_____

_____

_____

_____

WEATHER REPORT

MY RATING OF TODAY

☆ ☆ ☆ ☆ ☆

FAVORITE PART OF THE DAY

_____

_____

_____

CAMPING BUDDIES

MY CAMPING ADVENTURES
DAILY REPORT

CAMPSITE NAME AND LOCATION:

_____

DATE:

_____

TODAY'S ACTIVITIES

_____

_____

_____

_____

WEATHER REPORT

MY RATING OF TODAY

☆ ☆ ☆ ☆ ☆

FAVORITE PART OF THE DAY

_____

_____

_____

CAMPING BUDDIES

CAMPING DOODLES

MY CAMPING ADVENTURES
TRIP SUMMARY

ONE NEW THING I LEARNED DURING THIS CAMPING TRIP:

_____

MY FAVORITE ACTIVITY WAS:

_____

BEST THING I SAW:

BEST FOOD I ATE:

SOMETHING THAT MADE ME LAUGH!

THINGS I STILL WANT TO TRY NEXT TIME:

WHAT I WANT TO REMEMBER MOST WHEN I GET BACK HOME:

Camping Awards

FIRST UP IN THE MORNING	LAST UP IN THE MORNING
....	....

MARSHMALLOW MASTER	BEST CAMPFIRE STORY
....	....

FUNNIEST MOMENT	MOST EMBARRASSING MOMENT
....	....

BEST COOK	_____
....	....

_____	_____
....	....

GETTING READY

I AM GOING TO [ ]

I AM GOING TO BE CAMPING FOR [ ] DAYS.

COLOR IN THE DAYS YOU'LL BE CAMPING:

MONDAY	TUESDAY	WEDNESDAY	THURSDAY	FRIDAY	SATURDAY	SUNDAY
MONDAY	TUESDAY	WEDNESDAY	THURSDAY	FRIDAY	SATURDAY	SUNDAY

WHO IS GOING WITH US:

WE WILL CAMP IN A:

what will you take?

FLASHLIGHT

MAP OF CAMPSITE

COMPASS

HIKING BOOTS AND CLOTHES

WATER

CAMERA

WHISTLE

JOURNAL

FIRST AID KIT

SLEEPING BAG

LIST OTHER ITEMS YOU WANT TO REMEMBER TO PACK:

_____   _____

_____   _____

_____   _____

THINGS TO DO

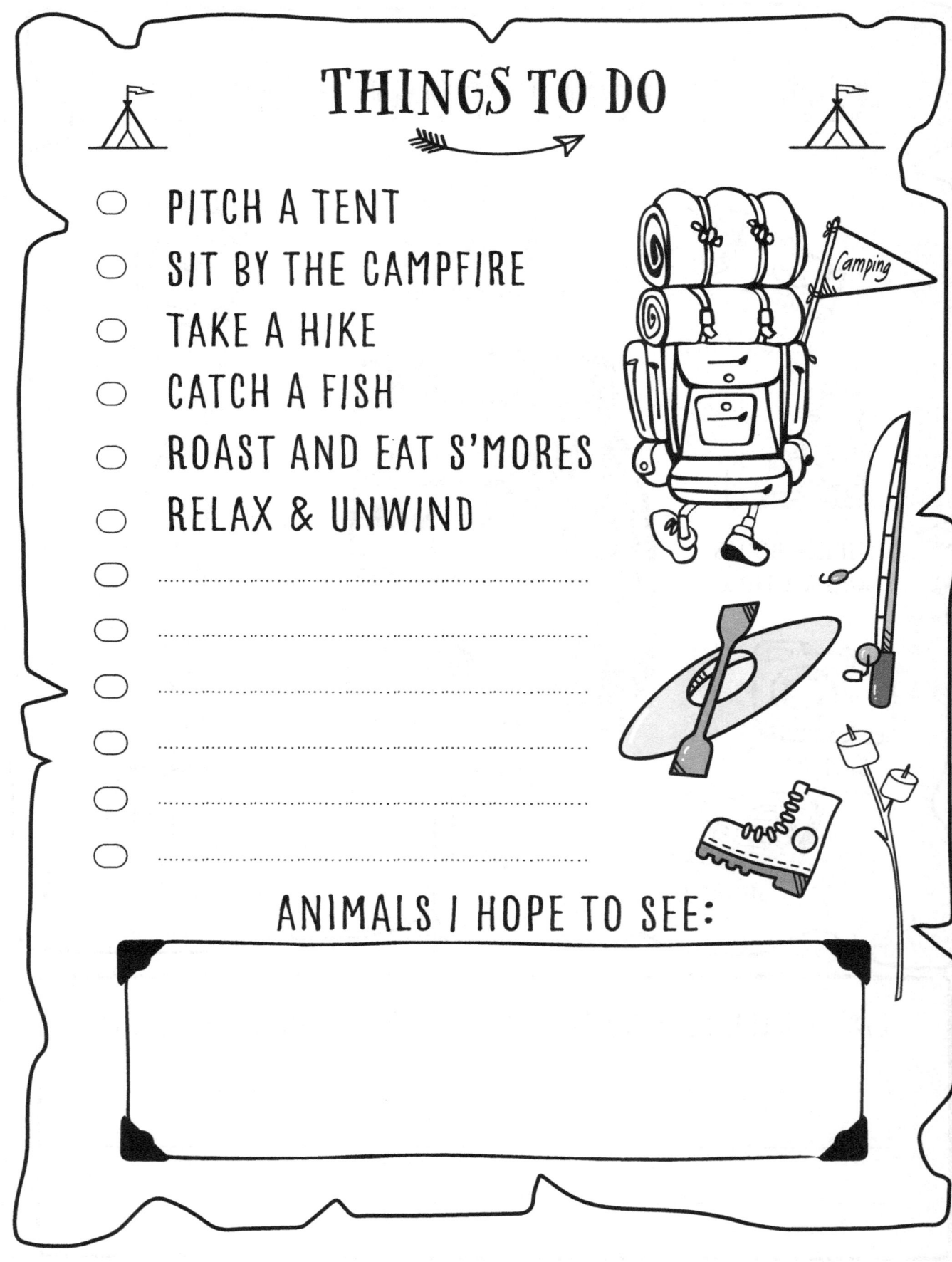

- PITCH A TENT
- SIT BY THE CAMPFIRE
- TAKE A HIKE
- CATCH A FISH
- ROAST AND EAT S'MORES
- RELAX & UNWIND
- ....
- ....
- ....
- ....
- ....
- ....

ANIMALS I HOPE TO SEE:

Safe Camping Rules

STAY TOGETHER

- STAY TOGETHER WITH YOUR GROUP.

- TELL A GROWN-UP YOUR LOCATION AT ALL TIMES.

- STAY ON THE MARKED TRAIL.

- ALWAYS WEAR YOUR WHISTLE, AND USE IT TO CALL FOR HELP IF YOU GET SEPARATED FROM YOUR GROUP.

STAY HEALTHY AND SAFE

- DON'T EAT ANY FRUITS OR PLANTS YOU FIND IN THE WILD BEFORE SHOWING IT TO A GROWN-UP.

- LEARN TO IDENTIFY COMMON POISONOUS PLANTS THAT MAY GROW IN YOUR CAMPING CLIMATE (SUCH AS POISON IVY AND POISON OAK). TAKE CARE TO AVOID THEM.

- WILD ANIMALS MAY LOOK CUTE AND CUDDLY, BUT NEVER TRY TO PET ONE.

- ASK YOUR CAMP LEADERS TO REVIEW FIRE SAFETY RULES EACH DAY. BE SURE TO PRACTICE THEM.

MY SAFE CAMPING NOTES

_____

_____

_____

_____

THINGS TO WATCH-OUT FOR IN OUR CAMPING AREA:

WATCH OUT!

Plants	Animals

Locations	Situations

camping Bingo

GET FOUR IN A ROW, UP, DOWN OR ACROSS, TO WIN

CAMPER	HOT COCOA	FLASHLIGHT	FROG
CAMP FIRE	TENT	MUSHROOMS	BINOCULAR
AXE	LIZARD	COMPASS	FISHING POLE
FISH	LOG	MARSHMALLOW FOR S'MORES	LANTERN

camping bingo

GET FOUR IN A ROW, UP, DOWN OR ACROSS, TO WIN

PINE TREE	TREE STUMP	OWL	AXE
FLASHLIGHT	CAMP SIGN	ACORN	CAMP FIRE
BINOCULAR	HIKING BOOT	MAPLE LEAF	CANOE
COMPASS	TENT	SQUIRREL	GRILL

camping Bingo

GET FOUR IN A ROW, UP, DOWN OR ACROSS, TO WIN

CAMPER	HOT COCOA	FLASHLIGHT	FROG
CAMP FIRE	TENT	FISH	BINOCULAR
CANOE	DEER	COMPASS	FISHING POLE
MUSHROOMS	LOG	MARSHMALLOWS	LANTERN

camping Bingo

GET FOUR IN A ROW, UP, DOWN OR ACROSS, TO WIN

HIKING BOOT	TREE STUMP	FIRST AID KIT	LANTERN
FLASHLIGHT	CAMP SIGN	ACORN	CAMP FIRE
BINOCULAR	TENT	BACKPACK	AXE
COMPASS	MAP	ANIMAL TRACKS	GRILL

DRAW (OR ATTACH)
A MAP OF THE CAMPSITE.

NATURE TREASURE HUNT

CAN YOU FIND?

- [ ] 2 ROCKS
- [ ] 1 LEAF
- [ ] 2 STICKS
- [ ] 3 FLOWERS
- [ ] 1 FEATHER
- [ ] 1 BARK
- [ ] 2 PINE-CONES
- [ ] 3 BERRIES

CAN YOU SEE?

- [ ] A BIRD
- [ ] A LIZARD
- [ ] A BUTTERFLY
- [ ] A DUCK
- [ ] AN INSECT
- [ ] A FISH

LOOK FOR SOMETHING WITH THE COLOR:

- [ ] GREEN
- [ ] YELLOW
- [ ] RED

camping selfie
SCAVENGER HUNT

GROUP SELFIE IN FRONT OF A LARGE TREE	GROUP SELFIE HOLDING PINE CONES	SELFIE WITH TWO KINDS OF STICKS
GROUP SELFIE ROASTING MARSHMALLOWS	GROUP SELFIE SITTING AROUND CAMP FIRE	GROUP SELFIE IN FRONT OF A LAKE
GROUP SELFIE IN FRONT OF A BOULDER	SELFIE STANDING ON A TREE STUMP	GROUP SELFIE IN FRONT OF A CAMP SIGN

MY CAMPING ADVENTURES
DAILY REPORT

CAMPSITE NAME AND LOCATION:

_____

DATE:

_____

TODAY'S ACTIVITIES

_____

_____

_____

_____

WEATHER REPORT

MY RATING OF TODAY

☆ ☆ ☆ ☆ ☆

FAVORITE PART OF THE DAY

_____

_____

_____

CAMPING BUDDIES

CAMPING DOODLES

NOTES AND PICTURES

MY CAMPING ADVENTURES
DAILY REPORT

CAMPSITE NAME AND LOCATION:

DATE:

_____ _____

TODAY'S ACTIVITIES

_____

_____

_____

_____

WEATHER REPORT

MY RATING OF TODAY

FAVORITE PART OF THE DAY

_____

_____

_____

CAMPING BUDDIES

MY CAMPING ADVENTURES
DAILY REPORT

CAMPSITE NAME AND LOCATION:

DATE:

_____

_____

TODAY'S ACTIVITIES

_____

_____

_____

_____

WEATHER REPORT

MY RATING OF TODAY

☆ ☆ ☆ ☆ ☆

FAVORITE PART OF THE DAY

_____

_____

_____

CAMPING BUDDIES

CAMPING DOODLES

MY CAMPING ADVENTURES
TRIP SUMMARY

ONE NEW THING I LEARNED DURING THIS CAMPING TRIP:

_____

MY FAVORITE ACTIVITY WAS:

_____

BEST THING I SAW:

BEST FOOD I ATE:

SOMETHING THAT MADE ME LAUGH!

THINGS I STILL WANT TO TRY NEXT TIME:

WHAT I WANT TO REMEMBER MOST WHEN I GET BACK HOME:

Camping Awards

FIRST UP IN THE MORNING	LAST UP IN THE MORNING
....	....

MARSHMALLOW MASTER	BEST CAMPFIRE STORY
....	....

FUNNIEST MOMENT	MOST EMBARRASSING MOMENT
....	....

BEST COOK	_____
....	....

_____	_____
....	....

Made in United States
North Haven, CT
16 June 2025

69886245R00070